1868 to 1948 to 2023:
The Journey of the Lives
and Gifts of All of These

SHE HAS A RIGHT

CHARLENE STRATTON

ISBN: 978-1-960136-29-9

Table of Contents

Dear Jason
        Brittney

Our Dear Neighbor Boy
Wish you the Best Holidays

        with Love

        Char Starke

        9-23-2023

Introduction

This is the journey of a child born to an unwed woman in 1948 and the pain the unwed woman had to bear, the judgment and the name calling. This is about the simple wisdom of my great grandfather Reinhart who was born three years after the civil war in 1868 and his gentle love, salvation, and lack of judgment. The journey continues through the Great Depression, acknowledging the community's ability to share with each other with whatever they had. In 1948 I came into the picture and this book chronicles the love of the people who came into my life, helped raise me, and the gifts and love given by them all.

So many are in my wreath of love—some for a day, some for a few years, and some for life. But they all are with me in my heart every day. The journey I have taken was possible due to the people who have loved me and helped shape me—they taught me that I had value. I am forever grateful for the miracles and divine intervention in my life. SHE HAS A RIGHT to not be punished and to be free of pain. It takes two to make a baby, and one pays the price.

1948. The war is over, and prosperity is coming back after WWII. Fashion is classy with hats and gloves, and the skirts were shorter due to war shortages. Nylons were rationed because silk was used for parachutes. Women wore dresses and skirts always with a full or half slip. Women had "house dresses" for working at home every day. Women dressed up to go shopping and when they went out in public or for going to dinner.

Men wore suits and fedora hats even to baseball games. Sneakers were just for P.E.

In 1948 the UN adopted the universal declaration of human rights. All humans are born free and with dignity. It was a time of nightclubs, with stage shows, linen tablecloths, men in suits, and women in dresses and hats. The movies were *I Remember Mama* and *Abbott and Costello Meet Frankenstein*. The most famous person was Bing Crosby, the funniest man was Jack Benny, and the most popular music artists were Perry Como, Dinah Shore, Doris Day, and Les Brown on guitar. Fashion hotties were Lana Turner, Rita Hayworth, and Ava Gardener. London hosted the Olympics, and Eliza Moore was the last known black slave. The United States was the first to recognize Israel as an independent state.

But women's rights had not changed much. They could vote since 1919, but financial rights were not out there for women. They had no credit rights unless they had a husband's signature, and they were under the thumb of a man's world, who had all the rights and were free to do as they chose.

When Joyce was in high school, the family moved to a small town in Wisconsin. Howard and his dad, Reinhert, had a sheet metal business in a building that was the first courthouse in Waushara County. In the small town, things were done pretty routinely and "how things should be done."

After high school, the toddling town of Chicago was calling her. That is where she thought she would find her hopes and dreams. The world was at her back door, and she was going to exit through that door. Secretarial or clerical work were the norm for women, and she got jobs just doing that. She was in the big city of fashion, night clubs, big bands, dancing, and dating.

Responsibility was not her forte. She would quit jobs or get fired for not showing up, so she had to rely on her sisters and parents for rent money so she could go on to the next job and the next party.

In 1948, her and her family's lives would change.

Her parents came from the Great Depression in Missouri. The government was helping people homestead with acreage in Missouri, so Reinhert, with his wanderlust, moved to a homestead in Missouri with his wife Lorena, his son Howard, and Howard's wife, Marie.

The Great Depression was terrible for the country, and the hardships were beyond huge.

Howard and Marie lived with his folks, Reinhert and Lorena, on the farm in Missouri at Turkey Ridge. They had a cow and chickens, which gave them milk, eggs, and meat. Howard had a small pension from being in the military which helped with the hardship of life. Most people ate beans every day and had no opportunity for betterment. Howard and a lot of the men dug ditches for 50 cents a day.

My mother told me stories about neighbors helping each other as they could, and mom and dad had neighbors come and get milk for their children and some eggs. Mom would make chicken dinner and have dad give some to neighbors as they could. One neighboring family had a very cruel, mean man who abused his wife and children. He would eat first, then the wife and kids. So mom took that meal to the family and told him if he wanted any, the wife and kids would eat first and then him, or he didn't get any at all. So he had to go by the rules mom laid down for him or he wouldn't get any.

Good for her!

Imagine what that woman and kids went through with him. Hopefully, they all learned from it, though I doubt it. But every time food went over to their place, the rules had to be followed by what Marie set for him or he didn't get any, and it continued that way.

The family gardened, canned the produce (and meat when they could), and the women made quilts.

Howard and Marie had three girls. The youngest was Joyce, who later became my birth mother.

Great grandpa Reinert Thompson was the inventor of a corn planter, a corn dryer, and was a tinsmith, now known as a sheet metal worker. Heating systems in schools were developed around 1909. His sheet metal work took him to Minnesota, Iowa, Illinois, and Wisconsin. He was an artist in copper work and made crosses for churches in many states, including the cross at Mt. Morris church. He also had something to do with contour farming, which is still practiced in the hills of southwestern Wisconsin. He loved the land and all it had to give. He wrote poetry and music, and he wrote a song about the winding gasconade river in Missouri. He wrote poems to and about his wife Lorena. He also had a little wanderlust. He was kind, gentle, and a God-fearing, loving man.

Years after Missouri, the family moved back to Wautoma, a small town in Wisconsin, and Reinert and Howard started the Thompson Sheet Metal business in a building that was the first courthouse in Waushara County. After the three girls were raised, Marie went to work at the mercantile store, which was unusual for most women at that time. But her life was about to change in 1948.

The Greek and the Baby

Joyce came from a time when women's place in the working world was always ruled and dominated by men, and their voices meant nothing. The flings meant something. They meant that women paid the price for the outcome of the fling, and were considered fallen women, and worse. The men were not called names or had any problem with shame.

If they got pregnant from their boss or boyfriend, the women were left to decide what they were going to do with no responsibility from the man. They were let go from their jobs. They didn't want people to find out. And it was the woman's fault! Their cries were not heard. They were ignored.

The suffering was theirs and theirs alone.

Joyce saw the trap so many of her friends were in, and she thought she would do better than that. But she needed to be needed, and the fun life took over. She went on dates with men who also just wanted a good time, and having fun ruled her life.

1948 was a big change for her. She met a Greek man who took her heart. He was handsome and fun. In those years, ethnic groups didn't cross too much. There were neighborhoods of German, Polish, Norwegian, Greek, etc. A lot of the time, Greek married Greek, so his family would not welcome her.

In 1948 she got pregnant with me. Now what? So she went back to the small town she came from to figure out what to do. In the small town, people would look at her with disgust, and the gossip was wild. She brought shame on her family. She ended up going to Chicago to the salvation army home for women like her! Her dad took her to the salvation army home and cried as he walked away.

They had the women work for their keep and punished them for getting themselves in that situation. There was a nurse at the salvation army home who had a relationship with a doctor, and she had to go there to have the baby and give it up for adoption. They didn't want people to know of this, and she paid the price as all the women did. Keep in mind, the men never never paid the price for this. NO responsibility for woman or child. They just went on with their lives as if nothing had happened. They had no hope for respect or hope of salvation. So the women were alone in their pain and hell and shamed for what THEY had done. Joyce never told the Greek lover of this until it was all over. They were done, and he went to Greece and married a Greek woman. Most women in that situation gave up the babies for adoption, and it was expected they would. The woman got pregnant, and the men left with no responsibility to the woman or child.

In September, I was born. Now what? They tried to talk Joyce into giving me up for adoption. Her baby was a beautiful, healthy, brown-haired baby and would be easy to adopt out and bring money. Joyce fought them on this and just refused. She just couldn't bear the thought of never seeing me again. So now she had to struggle alone with what to do to keep her baby and how she would do it.

It Takes Two to Make a Baby, And One Pays the Price

In September, I was born. Now what? Everybody tried and tried to talk her into giving me up for adoption, as I was a beautiful little girl and easy to adopt out for good money. She fought them on this and just couldn't do it. So now she had to struggle alone with what to do and how to keep her baby.

While at the Salvation Army home, she went to see her baby girl, and she told the staff, "Don't point her out to me. I know what she looks like because an angel showed me my baby." She was right! I don't know how or who helped her, but it must have been divine intervention. The nurse was amazed at her story.

Everyone wanted her to give me up for adoption. This was a baby that would go quick and bring in money. She fought this battle alone and wouldn't give me up and had to find a way to keep me.

She found this wonderful lady named Helen who took in and cared for babies like me. Keep in mind, things were so different then and this was a place that women could work and have their child taken care of. They had to pay her, and the care was excellent because she loved the children. Helen also cared for an older man named Dell who lived with her, and Dell was a kind and good man. Helen lived her life giving to others. She had a bad foot, and was not wealthy by any means, but her heart was pure and she actually ended up raising a little girl whose mother never came back.

She became her daughter.

For three years, I lived with my wonderful foster mother and Dell, and I had a pet crow and an iron fenced-in yard. I was well taken care of. There is a special place in heaven for this wonderful lady who gave her life for so many.

Joyce was not paying Helen, and something had to happen to this three year old child. But what? And of course, there was no financial help from the father of the child. When you don't go to work, party, and shop, the money doesn't go for the care of the child. Now something had to be done. She went home and talked to her parents (my grandparents) about adopting me.

Joyce's parents struggled with what to do. What would people say and how would the family react to this?

My great grandfather and great grandmother lived in the same town a few blocks away. My great grandfather Reinhert was one of the most kind, loving men, wrote poetry to and about his wife and a song about the Winding Gasconade river in Missouri. He was gentle and came from a Norwegian family. His mother came from the Selsegn farm in Norway which has been in our family since the 1600s, and gave birth to my great grandfather in Mt. Morris where the Norwegians settled in a log cabin in 1868. The hardships they had were great, and Grandpa Reinhert became the oldest of the family. His parents buried his three sisters a few days apart after they died from typhoid, and they think the only reason that Reinhert survived was because he was nursing.

Reinhert was a man ahead of his time in inventing machinery. I was also told he had something to do with contour farming which is still being used in hilly land farming in the southwest part of Wisconsin. He loved God, nature, family, creating, and writing and was never judgemental of people.

Reinhert's son and his wife, my grandparents, went to see him and talk to him about what to do with the three year old girl, and Reinhert said, in all his wisdom and love, "SHE HAS A RIGHT TO HER FAMILY." That was the answer they and I needed. He was ahead of his time! No one had ever said or thought this except for him.

So my grandparents went in the old gray Dodge car and went to Chicago to get this little girl. The roads were not like now, and it was a long trip but they had the answer and knew it was right.

A Goodbye and a Hello

My foster mom, Helen, had me all dressed up to meet the new people. She had me serve cookies and talk with them. I was in a fancy dress with my hair curled. She must have told me that this was my grandparents, as I went and sat on grandpa's lap who would soon be dad's lap and rubbed his bald head.

Soon after the cookies and time to talk and get to know each other, we started loading up the gray Dodge with my things. I had a pet hamster in a cage, and Helen must have told me I was going to my grandparents' because the car was loaded with the hamster on top of it all in his cage. I don't remember saying goodbye to Helen, but Dell wasn't there because he couldn't bear saying goodbye to me. I never saw him again, but he gave me something that I hold dear to my heart and always will. He played guitar and would sing YOU ARE MY SUNSHINE my only sunshine. I had a clear plastic record of him singing that and a little girl giggling in the background. It was me! I never realized that until I was an adult. You are my sunshine is my favorite song, and I love Dell. He has a special place in my heart.

On the way to my new home, we stopped at every ice cream place and got ice cream. Now that was highly rare for grandpa to do this, as he wasn't the kind of man to spoil a child. He was stern and brought up in a different time, and he believed children should be seen and not heard. But he was breaking all the rules for me so I would ease into my new life with them.

We got home to our small town and they lived upstairs of the legion home in town. They got me and my hamster (who's name was Hamper) settled in. My bedroom had wallpaper of dancing girls and boys. I had a swing on a big tree and played by the creek, made friends, and was settling into my new life with people who loved me—I was doing well. I didn't think of my foster mom or Dell until years later.

We lived in the upstairs of the legion home. There would be gatherings of the legion men, and I would always peek around and watch as they played games, ate, smoked, and drank.

We lived next door to a lady and her husband who had no children, so she loved being with me. I remember she had a doll that she treated like a baby. We went to the store in town that had children's clothes and bought clothes for the doll. She even had a crib for this baby doll. She could not have children, and her husband wouldn't LET HER adopt any. How sad. SHE HAD THE RIGHT to have a child, but he gave her no right. One Christmas, they got a child from an orphanage to have Christmas with and buy toys for, but then they had to go back! It was cruel. They always enjoyed my company, and I would eat with them sometimes with my cousin Bob. But that's all she could do.

My grandparents adopted me so I would not be taken away at the whim of Joyce. I am so thankful for that. I have no idea what my life would have been like with her, but I know it would not have been good at all. SO FROM NOW ON, THEY WERE MOM AND DAD.

A few years later, we moved to a bigger house in town and my grandparents moved in with us. They had their own living room and bedroom. So I had a few years of knowing Reinhert, this wonderful loving man who said SHE HAS A RIGHT to her family. Great grandpa always wore a suit with a vest and a watch on a chain in his vest pocket. He was tall, thin, and gentle. We would go for walks, he would hold my hand, and we talked. I don't remember what we talked about, but I have a feeling our conversations were full of his wise words and guidance.

My great grandmother was not the warm loving person Reinhert was. She was more stern and never really showed me much affection or gave me much time.

My great grandfather got very sick. I was so young and had no idea what happened, but it was a stroke. They let me in to see him once, and ten days later, he passed. The man who believed SHE HAD A RIGHT was gone from my life. He is still with me in so many ways. I have his copper work and my kids do, too. I have his poems and a gift from him a lady gave me that I treasure.

One day, mom told me we were going to a lady's house for tea and that she wanted to meet me. She lived by the old Dafoe school. Grandpa's brother Carl roomed there. So mom and I went to see her, and we had cookies and tea. She had braids that were wrapped around her head and was dressed in a dress and old shoes. She was very nice to me and I sat very politely as I was taught to by mom and Helen. I was even taught to curtsey from Helen.

A little while later, the lady said, "I have a gift for you." Wow, that was exciting. She brought out this box all wrapped up and gave it to me. I very carefully opened it and in the box were wooden oxen with the yoke around them pulling a cart. She told me grandpa Reinhert hand-carved these four years ago for his brother when he was sick. Under the cart reads *Made by Reinhert to Torge 1888 and Charlene 1955*. I was six or seven then. I cried and put them away and never played with them to keep them safe. I still have them in a special place. What a gift of love that is still giving.

I never saw the woman again. It's amazing how people come into your life for just a moment and have a special place in the wreath of love.

Now I'm growing up with friends both boys and girls. I got a new bike with training wheels and that was freedom! I rode it every day and enjoyed my new freedom exploring town with friends and making new ones.

One day, dad told me I had to learn to ride without training wheels, or he was going to take my bike back to the store. YIKES! So now I had to get help. The neighbor across the street had twin grandsons. I told them my plight and they helped me learn to ride without training wheels. Life was good again.

Mom and dad had a garden, and life was pretty routine. Monday was wash day, Tuesday ironing, canning, and daily work. We lived close to the railroad tracks and most days my friends and I would go watch the train and wave at the man in the caboose. He would always wave back. I wonder what his name was. Then we would hop on our bikes and go on to the next adventure.

A few years later, we moved to the boulevard and my dad's brother and mother moved in with us. I loved living on the boulevard with new friends, and it was a busy neighborhood.

There were families with seven kids, others four, and I had a friend who lived down the street and we walked to school together. Another one of my friends came to his grandmother's in summer and we would go to her cottage on the lake and fish, swim, and have fun.

Down around another street was a friend who was a bully, and one day I had enough and punched him in the face, knocking his glasses off, and things changed from that time on and we are dear friends.

Behind our house was a field, and the neighborhood would play baseball and, on summer nights, shadow tag, hide and seek, starlight moonlight, Annie Annie over, human chains and, yes, hula hoops. I still love them all and they are in my heart and my wreath of love.

Family came up from Chicago and other parts of Illinois to spend a few days with mom, dad, me, and grandma and uncle Rein. My birth mom Joyce's sister and family came up, and my cousins and I played and fought and played some more. My cousins, Bob, Tom, and Susan and I became like siblings more than cousins, and to this day still are.

My birth mother would come up with her latest boyfriend every so often and spend a weekend before going back to the life of whatever fun was next. A lot of times she would use her venom on family and me. She never stopped this habit of venom and lies. Mom, dad, and family members bailed her out financially through the years A LOT. I remember mom and dad wiring her money so she wouldn't get kicked out of her apartment.

Sometimes when she came home, she had friends in town she would go and see and I would go with her to play with their kids. I remember one friend of hers, who was a beautiful woman, had a fire engine red '57 Thunderbird convertible and yellow telephone! I had never seen that! All phones were black, but hers was yellow and I asked her if I could call mom just so I could talk on the yellow phone. I said, "When I grow up, I'm going to have a yellow phone." AND I DID.

Joyce and the other family members never really helped mom with meals, dishes, or anything else. I never understood how they could have mom wait on them as she aged, and I always felt mom HAD THE RIGHT to be more than the idea that her place in life was to do household chores. She had grandma, Rein, and a kid to take care of. She had a lot on her plate. But through it all, she was the most wonderful loving lady, and she loved me with all she had. I love her with all I have still. She told me stories of Norway and her growing up. At the age of 15, she came over from Norway to her dad's cousin on a farm. She could speak no English and had to learn the language and money and the ways of America. The family on the farm had lost their daughter prior to her arrival in America, and so she became their daughter instead. She helped fill the void in their hearts, and Marie played guitar and she played on the lost daughter's guitar. I now have that guitar. It came through the family and was treasured.

Teen Years

I was raised on Lefse and Norwegian cookies, always home cooking. Mom made the best pies. To this day I can't copy her.

Now we are a teenager and again life is changing. Camp Waushara was the place to be. Live rock and roll bands. Jerry Lee Lewis, Doctor Bop, and the headliners, The Rivieras, Bad Boy, and Roemans, to name a few. Dance floor, 18 year old beer bar and 21 adult bar. Kids from all over came to camp, Milwaukee, Berlin, and other towns in the county, and it was a special time that will never be again. Dick Clark's Hitsville show came to camp. When I got there, my old-friend-turned-bully came to me and told me there was a man looking for me. I had no idea what that was about, and my friend was going to protect me from him. Finally this man came up to me and asked me if I was Char. I said yes, and he told me who he was. I was so glad to see him. He was a fireman years ago in Chicago that had gone with Joyce, and he was always nice. Now retired, he drove the bus for Dick Clark's Hitsville show. He got me back with the stars, and I got autographs and talked with them, and I had a lot of friends that night who wanted to come with me. A few were let in. I am so glad I saw him, and we talked, and it was good. I never saw him again, but what a special time it was.

Mom and dad's house was buzzing with my friends, food, and the phone ringing a lot. You know, girls calling and the drama of life. I'm sure that helped keep them young.

There was a place downtown that the teens hung out for burgers and soda and smoking. We would walk there often. The jukebox going, and we were of course cool. Big hair that was in big rollers, teased, and sprayed to a fare thee well.

One night my friend and I were getting fries and soda when these guys walked in from school, and I had not ever seen this one guy. He was handsome, and I was twitterpated. And he was too. When my friend and I walked home that night, I told her that was the guy I was going to marry. That was also the time I started having strength and was changing again. I dropped a few friends who treated me nasty at their whim, changed friends, and started a new adventure in life.

It's amazing how life gives you things you never expected, and so good. And again, life changed. Of course I had to call my other dear friend Margie right away. He was handsome and different from what I had known before, and the new adventure began.

We started dating and going to Camp Waushara, movies, and out with friends. It was an on-again-off-again relationship. We both came from different worlds. He came from farming, hard work, and a big family, and I was a young woman raised in town without hard labor. He was into farming and cars, and I was into fashion and girl stuff. Cars were a passion for guys, and Roger was one of them. He had Chevys and worked jobs to have them.

There was Eight Ball Hall and Milty Wilty, where we also hung out and kids gathered.

We had to learn about each other's worlds and we enjoyed them both.

One summer, my cousin from Norway came. Tone came with uncle Berger and spent the summer with us. I spent my summer with her and showed her my world and friends. We became very close, and Roger too. Now mom had two girls in her house and we showed uncle Berger and Tone around and had relatives come up, and we all had a great time sharing our lives. Treasured memories.

That summer, Rog and I decided to get married, and I wanted Tone to be in our wedding, so we planned a wedding quickly, as her visa was going to end. We had the reception out at Roger's folks' farm. A week later, Tone had to leave. It was a very sad time for both of us, but she had a man back home and was glad to go on to her new adventure.

We lived next door to Roger's folks, as they had a small house on their farm. We fixed it up some. A year later, John was born. He was premature but strong. He had to be in the hospital until he got to five pounds. My family had not had a baby in years, so the whole family came up that Christmas and went to the hospital to spend time with the cutest baby boy. We finally got him home, and I was busy being a mom and learning all the new adventures of it. We went to mom and dad a lot, as they just loved their grandson and wanted to be with him. We had a lot of weddings to go to because all our friends were getting married and life was changing. It was also the Vietnam war, when boys were getting drafted and were sent to the hell of war right out of high school.

We went on with life, and I saw some things that made me question why women accepted being treated in the ways they were. Women had house parties of Tupperware, clothes, house decorations, etc. I was invited to a friend's party and asked my other friend if she wanted to go with me. She did, and when the day came, I went to pick her up. She was all dressed and ready to go and HAD to go to the barn and ask her husband if she could go. HE said No. And she didn't go! SHE HAD A RIGHT to be treated better!

Our Son and the Farm

Our son was born over a year later. He was premature but strong. He was the cutest baby, and the sun rose and set on him. Now I am a mom! He was the first baby in my family in years, and that Christmas, the whole family came home and we all went up to the hospital to see the baby. He just had to get up to five pounds before he could come home. There were a lot of presents for him, and family on both sides sent gifts for our little baby John.

Roger's dream since the age of five was to own the farm down the road from his parent's farm. He knew them all his life, and they couldn't farm anymore. They wanted us to buy it, and we went through the process of buying the farm. John was two and a half.

I had NO clue about farming, the work, the finances of it all, or even how to drive a tractor or what the machinery was or how to use it. Now my life was changing again. I was pregnant with our second son. Paul was premature and not strong. Here is where the miracle started. Marshfield had just opened its prenatal wing a week prior to his birth. Doctor Porter had his first run to save a baby from Marshfield and came in a fire ambulance, because Paul had to be in a special incubator and the fire ambulance had the hook-up for it. There were only three in the state at that time and two were full.

The doctor worked on Paul for two hours before he could go in the ambulance. The firemen were standing watch and didn't know Roger was the father, and they said the baby wouldn't make it from the hospital to the ambulance!

I was put in a room far away from the nursery, and I cried and prayed. I never prayed for anything so hard in my life as I did for our son to be okay and for God to let us have him.

All of a sudden, I got the biggest peace. I stopped crying, and I knew Paul would be okay.

When I saw the doctor, I told him of my experience. He said when they were on the way to Marshfield, they were swerving between deer and on their way to save him. The doctor said he didn't know if it was the juggling of the ambulance or what, but Paul started breathing better, and he was going to be okay. My experience and what happened in the ambulance were at about the same time. The doctor agreed it was God's hand in this.

When I went to Marshfield to see Paul, I said to the nurse, "He doesn't even know I'm here." She said, "Oh yes he does. I'll show you." He was lying on his tummy facing away from me. She went on the side he was facing, and I was on the other side. We both started talking to him at the same time, and He turned his head to me! I cried. She said he knew my voice when I carried him. What a gift to me and my son!

We were moving to our farm with our two and a half year old son and the other son at

Marshfield hospital. My in-laws helped with getting us set up with some dairy cattle and getting things ready for milking cows. My mom and birth mom helped me clean the big old farm house. I also made trips to Marshfield to see my son who was improving all the time.

We started our farming and work every day, and the day came when we could go to Marshfield and get our son. That was in August 1970. I wrote a letter to the doctor thanking him for saving our son and for all he did. Three years later, when they had a party for the kids that were there, we took him and I wanted to see the doctor. The doctor thanked me for the letter. He said we were the only ones who thanked him for saving our baby.

A Few Years Later

Our place was always busy with 365 days of milking, feeding, manure handling, births, and machinery repair. Our place was called Grand Central with neighbors, friends, family, and salesmen with seed, oil, fuel, and other people involved in agriculture. Coffee was always going, and we had Kool-Aid for kids. I counted 15 kids in the yard. It was constant food and coffee. I hardly ever cooked for the five of us, it was always six or more.

One mother's day, when everyone else was going to dinner, I was out picking rocks out of the field with my two boys for planting. That day I felt like my worth was nothing. NO card. No celebration of my being a woman or mother. Just slave labor.

After the day was done, my husband asked me what was for supper, and I blew up. I said I was taking my boys to A&W for supper for a treat and he could starve, and I slammed the door. I thought I broke the window in it. That was another moment I HAD THE RIGHT to be treated right. It never happened again, and my husband was so sorry for that time. Roger and I both learned a lesson. You can't let work take over other things in your life.

But farming was very demanding in many ways. The crops had to be in on time, weather was always a factor, and there were always surprises along the way, and not usually good ones.

I helped with the fieldwork, raked hay, chopped hay, picked rocks, disced fields, and then there was laundry, meals, and housework, and dishes to be done at the end of the day. I didn't get the help inside, so I was doing dishes at nine or ten at night. Needless to say, it wasn't always caught up, and things were not as they should be.

On New Year's Day in 1975, our beautiful daughter came into the world, Jennifer Marie. She was full term, and again the family was overjoyed at having a girl in the family. Her middle name was after her grandma. She was so close to mom, and loved being with her. She was a beautiful little girl and such a loving child. I remember one day, when she was having a nap in our bedroom, she came out and told me that Jesus just came and saw her. I asked her what he said. Jenny told me he just said nothing, he just stretched out his arms and let her know he loved her. I don't doubt her, and I told her this is beyond beautiful and how blessed she was. And this has stayed with her. You never forget those moments. What a beautiful miracle. A child's heart is always open.

The years and days went on as usual now we were expanding the herd and had more work. In the vicious circle of farming, the work takes over your time and thinking of your worth as a person, and it happens to the men too. After a while, your worth is in your work. You get lost. But you keep going and going.

Jenny was nine months old when Roger's dad died suddenly. Now our lives had changed in just a few minutes. The cows at his folks' farm and our farm had to be milked. Now there were two farms to take care of, and the feeding, manure, milking, and fieldwork was overwhelming! We hired a man to milk over at his folks' farm and tried to keep everything going. We were beyond any sense of leisure time. Roger's mom wanted to stay in her home, so we made a deal to buy the cows, pay taxes for the farm, and run both farms and get a hired man to help with all this. So the cows came over to our farm, and the expansion began with tons of work. We built a free stall barn and remodeled the barn from stanchion to milking parlor.

A dear friend of ours, Steve, invented a crowd gate for us to help move the cows from the free stall barn into the milking parlor. Steve and Barb and the kids were like family. One time when they were here, they and the kids got snowed in with us for three days. That time when we milked, we had to dump it because the milkman couldn't come and pick it up for the creamery.

Now the farm was expanding with more land, more work, 365 days constant.

In the 1980s dairy was changing. There was a glut on the market for milk. So the government started to tax the farmers for producing milk. Our taxes were $1000.00 a month! So what did the farmers have to do to survive? They expanded the herds to help offset the heavy taxes. They took our means of living away. Now the government realized this wasn't working, and it was a huge mistake. So they came up with the herd buyout. You had to put in your bid for them to pay you to stop milking. We put in our bid, and it was accepted. The rule was the farmer couldn't have any cattle of any kind for five years. We were the biggest dairy in the county. Now the trucks came to haul the cows. We loaded all 175 heads, and they all had to go to slaughter.

That was a very hard and sad day. It's easy to sit behind a desk and make rules and know nothing about what you are making rules for. I always wondered where the tax money went and what it was used for. I never got the answer.

Now the dairy is done, and life had changed and wasn't the continual grind. Now what would happen to me? I had no job experience or any skills that I knew of besides my life of farming. I had given all I had to my family, friends, and our heart kids.

I saw an ad for a tutor at a school, and my life changed again.

I made a lot of good friends with the kids' parents. Their kids were out here a lot, and they all had a good time. They had to help with chores just like our kids, and then they had their freedom and play. They built forts and rode motorcycles. We had over 300 acres for them to have room to play. They would come home from school and hit the refrigerator and eat tons before supper. Thank goodness I had a freezer full of meat. And I went grocery shopping a lot. But we enjoyed all the kids, and they all have a special place in our hearts. The parents always knew their kids were safe and had fun here.

One girl, Michelle, came out with her brothers and she was a little older than Jenny. She was a kind of big sister. Our other friends had a daughter, Nichole, who was younger than Jennifer, and Jenny became a big sister to her. Our heart kids are Steve, Mark, Nichole, Tim, Scott, Michelle, Art, Randy, Nanette, Bridgette, and Ron.

When Jennifer was in eighth grade, she had a Halloween party out in the barn. The kids had food, music, and a hayride with prize money hidden in the hay. They had to look through and pull apart the hay for the prize money. They had so much fun doing that. The parents had to pick them up around 11:00. I had some parents out here helping me. The kids said they had the best time and it was good for all.

One summer after the farm was expanded, all the boys were doing chores. I will never know who started it, but someone threw manure at someone, and then the game was on. Manure and afterbirth were the weapons. When the fight was over, they THOUGHT they were going to come into the house. I stopped them at the door and told them to go out to the windmill and strip down to their underwear and rinse off their clothes. So they were out there cleaning up the mess, and one boy said, "BOY, YOUR MOM IS CRABBY."

We had neighbors' kids who came and shared our life and memories. Later they moved to Missouri. We had nephews and nieces come to the farm a lot, too, and share our lives. Our farm gave so many memories and good work ethic to so many kids, and it holds a special place in their hearts, and they still love to come and see us. This is so wonderful.

All the heart kids.

Kids Growing Up and Dad

The kids were growing up, and graduations began. We had graduation parties for the kids and made food for 100 people or more. Our oldest son went into the air force. He said his goodbyes to mom and dad. We took him to Milwaukee airport, and he was on to a new adventure. I cried most of the way home. When we got home, our phone was ringing, and my friend Mary told me that dad was not good and mom wouldn't call the ambulance until we got there. Mary had been with them all day. Mom had called her not knowing what to do. So we tore into town, and when we got there, dad was just sitting in his pajamas and not responding to anything or anyone. We called the ambulance and he ended up at the Vets home. I think he shut down because he knew he wouldn't see John again after he joined the air force. He passed on their 65th wedding anniversary.

Mom was alone now and she spent a lot of time with us, and we were in touch every day. We would talk about many things; about her childhood in Norway and her mom and dad. One day she told me when they lived in Missouri, she had fallen and had a baby stillborn because of the fall. She had dark hair and was beautiful.

Mom said, "I guess I was supposed to have a dark hair girl after all." Mom said, "I never named her." This haunted mom all these years, and SHE HAD A RIGHT to have a name. So I told mom let's name her NOW! Let's pray for God to give her a name. I asked mom what her name would have been. She said she wanted to give her a Norwegian name, Borghild. So we held hands and I said a prayer for God to give her this name. This gave mom so much peace, and it didn't haunt her anymore.

Now the kids were gone, and life had changed for us again. We were empty nesters.

Paul went to work in Waunakee, and Jennifer went on to college at La Crosse. Then time went on and the kids came home to visit and we were with our adult kids.

Special Education

Later in the 80s, I went to work as a tutor at a school that got a grant to have tutors to help with kids' learning. I loved it and all the people I worked with. What a whole new experience for me. When you teach, you also learn. I loved every minute of it.

I knew the grant was going to come to an end. I saw an ad for a teacher's aide. I had no typewriter, so I just wrote my application by hand; I got called, and got the job. So I tutored in the morning and worked as an aide in the afternoon until I put my two weeks in and stayed as the aide at the other school. The teacher had all the kids write me a goodbye note. I cried all the way to the other school and started my new adventure.

I got my license as a special ed paraprofessional and loved it. Like I said before, when you teach, you learn and grow too. I helped the kids with work. We would sit around the table and read, work, and learn. We also made a bond by doing this, and they learned to trust me, and we would talk about many things. I held them when they were sobbing because their dog died, they had family issues, friends, and happy moments.

Now just like any place I guess there were the nasty coworkers who are jealous and enjoy being nasty, but most were good and still are friends with their coworkers. The other wonderful part is I still hear from some of the kids and have gone to their weddings, out to eat, baby showers, and graduations. They have done well. What I find interesting is the people they are in touch with aren't the teachers. It's the aides, janitors, cooks, etc. who were important. Another lesson learned.

I have a sleigh with the flowers just like he had them that I put out every Christmas and a plaque one of my students made for me. I found out he was homeless at the time. That is why we do what we do. Another lesson.

I left after my kids graduated. I did third grade through high school. I knew it was changing, and it was not going to be the same. So I left and went on to other things. But I hold the kids in my heart.

I had a couple of girls that were my students, and I tried to give them hope and make them realize they were smart and HAD THE RIGHT to be treated well and have a good life.

I went to one of my student Samantha's graduation from Madison and she invited me to her party. When I got there, I saw three tables full of awards and the cords for all she had accomplished. I was just amazed and so proud of her. I told her I was so proud and she was awesome. She said, "Mrs. Stratton, you always told me I could." I never forgot that, and now she is married and has a wonderful life and kids. I went to her wedding and showers.

Another one of my wonderful girls, Rebecca, I hear from a lot. She is smart and beautiful, and I went to her wedding. She has a son and is working hard. I see her once in a while, and we have gone out to eat together, and I still love her. She told me once I was the reason that some of them looked forward to coming to school. I never knew that and hold that dear to my heart.

You never really know the influence you have on someone. But it is so good to know. And we need to know.

We had exchange students, and I tried to get to know them and their cultures. There were two girls from South Korea, and I would talk with them and we had a great relationship.

I never understood why the school has exchange students and never have them speak to the whole high school and tell of their countries and culture. There is so much to learn from each other. After they went back, I got a gift from one of the girls in the mail, and I treasure it.

I did some waitressing. I met a lot of great people and made new friends. I enjoyed it, and then I decided it was time to retire and enjoy other adventures. I could enjoy the grandkids now and share life with them all. A lot of them had graduated and were going on with their lives, and I treasure our time with them. And now we are great grandparents, and time marches on.

It was our 25th wedding anniversary and the kids were home, as were some of our heart kids. I went into town to get mom and bring her out to celebrate with us all. When I went to the apartment, I noticed the drapes were drawn, and I knew something was wrong. I got that awful scared feeling as I went in. I found mom on the floor, unable to move. I called the ambulance and then called home. Roger and the kids were there before the ambulance. They took her to Berlin, and we all went to the hospital.

The nurse came out and told us we could go and see her, but her heart was not good. I remember telling the nurse, "Let the kids go in and see her, and you will see what her heart is made of." They went in and held her hand and talked with her, and her heart was doing better. The nurse was amazed.

Mom ended up crippled and had to be put in a nursing home. One day when I was there to see her, she said, "Guess who came to see me." So I guessed and finally gave up. She said Leola, her best friend in Missouri who had passed several years ago. I said to mom, "What did she say?"

"She said she would see me soon."

I knew time was short. I asked mom what the best years of her life were. She said, "When I was in Missouri, I was the poorest but I learned the most." I never forgot that. Lesson learned.

She passed a few weeks later in 1992.

Joyce had moved here from Chicago after her abusive boyfriend passed, and now she was in my life and our family's lives more. I tried to have a relationship with her, but she had to do her venom on me and more lies and games of her choosing.

After mom's passing, I would go every Thursday after work and have supper with Joyce and get her groceries and help her out. It went well and seemed to be going in the right direction. She was never good with money, had big overdraft fees at the bank, and had her power shut off for not paying the bill for months. I have no idea what she did with her money. I had to be POA and resolve the bank mess and the power company. I got the mess cleaned up, and things were going well.

Our twin grandsons were born in 1991! They were our biggest joy, and mom got to see them and love them before she passed. Our beautiful daughter-in-law got to know mom.

The kids were at the farm most weekends, and the twins grew up on the farm, and we had such treasured special times. Then along came their sister and more joy and treasured times.

Paul and Bobbi married in Saxeville and were busy after the kids came. Our oldest son John and soon-to-be daughter-in-law, Peg, got married in 1999 and had their reception here on the farm. Rog and John blacksmithed and forged three pairs of floor-standing candle holders for the wedding, so her folks, us, and them could each have a pair from the wedding. It was a lot of work to get the barn ready, but so worth it. The barn was dressed up beautifully and people said we should have had wedding magazines to show this, it was so beautiful. A friend of mine from work was getting married a few weeks after our son, and she was having trouble getting a place for a reception. I told her the barn is ready, so come and use it and decorate how you choose. It was another great day and time. And it really helped them out. We never charged them for it, we just wanted to help them out.

In 2000, the next year, our daughter and soon-to-be son-in-law, Nate, got married here, so we had another wedding to prepare for. Again it was beautiful. One of our extra kids made a beautiful cake and some of the food. Roger made iron hooks for the lanterns that graced the aisle of the tent they were getting married in on the farm. It was beautiful and everyone had a good time and loved how the barn was, and of course, our beautiful daughter.

When Randy got married, he also had his reception on the farm. So it has had a lot of special moments and memories.

Some of the other events that were on the farm were 60s reunions for all the 60s people from school. I thought it would be fun to get people through the years from school. When you have friends from other classes and years, you never get to see them if you only have a class reunion. So I created this out at the farm and did it for several years. It was a lot of work and a lot of fun. I had 45s hanging from the beams and random pictures from annuals posted all over. It was casual, and everyone really enjoyed it. We saw friends from years ago that had moved, and we connected again. The first year I had Lenny and Joan from Camp Waushara out and teachers too, because they were all a big part of our lives. We all toasted Lenny and Joan, raised our glasses, and said thanks for the memories. He said it was so good to see his kids! I'm so glad I did that. A few years later he was gone. Gatherings are good. They bring family and friends together and make memories. So important.

We have had relatives from Norway here, and that was such a special time. We had gatherings for them, made the bond across the ocean and shared family, and made more memories and love.

All times and memories that are so treasured by all.

Grand Children

Now we had twin grandsons, Jordan and Joshua, and later Taylor Marie, who was also named after mom. So my cousin (sister), my daughter, and granddaughter all carry her name. What a tribute to her. They were here most weekends and grew up on the farm.

John and Peg's son, Colin, came up here as often as he could and loves to help on the farm. Jenny and Nate have Elliott and Esri. When Elliott was little, he loved to make bread with me, and Esri is beautiful inside and out and wise. Both are so smart. Each one has their own personality and are all so special. We are blessed with them. They are grown now. The sun rose and set on all the kids. I love being with them.

We are now great grandparents, and again there is change. Through the years, the Christmases, Easters, birthdays, and all the special moments, I hope the grandkids hold in their hearts and always remember THEY HAVE THE RIGHT! I hope we gave them something to hold on to as their lives change.

The grandsons have learned the art of blacksmithing from grandpa, and some of their friends have learned from him as well. We also have extra grandkids from our heart kids. What a blessing they all are.

And there will always be gatherings of just being and food and fun. We had friends from England who were in the USA for a couple of years with a business. They were up most weekends with the kids. Some of their friends and parents from England came. Again more special times and memories. Such special times we hold in our hearts. We are so blessed to have them all in our lives, that they were all here, and we all shared such special times and love.

Time goes on, and with all the love.

When I was 29, I met my Greek father for the first time. I really wanted to know the other side of me. I knew the Norwegian side but not the Greek side of me. Joyce arranged the meeting with him. She contacted him and told him I wanted to meet him. No intention of hurting anyone, just to meet him. So we set the day for this to happen.

We went to my Greek father's restaurant and I saw him for the first time. His brother from California was there too. He was the only one in their family who knew about me.

Unusual timing or divine timing? Tom, the brother who knew about me, was there from California at that time and saw me too. George, my birth dad, was a little stand-offish at first, but then his brother Tom came over and talked to me and wondered who I was because I looked familiar. I told him who I was. He then told me he knew Joyce.

We talked for a long time, and then I went up to George and started to talk to him. I told him I wasn't there to hurt anyone, not there for money, and that I just wanted to meet him. I asked him if he ever thought about me. He looked away for a second and then said yes. And we went on from there.

We talked for a while. I told him about my family, our farm, and our wonderful kids. As we talked, he realized there was nothing to fear. I was at the counter talking with him when HIS son, my half-brother, came in to work with his dad. I sat there trying to burn his face in my memory. I was just a customer as far as he knew, and I left it that way.

We later decided to go for lunch and coffee the next day. I was looking forward to this time with them both and getting to know and learn about them.

I was with Joyce that night at her place. She lived with a terrible, horrible, controlling, jealous man, and of course, she told him what was happening and why I was there, so he was mean. Right now, I'm being nice about how EVIL he was. He had connections, if you know what I mean, and he was a lowlife scum, an insult to scum. And I'm still being nice.

That night I woke up to the scum yelling, humiliating, swearing, and threatening Joyce. I let it go for a bit to see if she would stand up to him or if he would stop. After 10 minutes of this continuing, I got up and marched out to the kitchen where he was doing his evil. She was at the table with her head down, and he just kept on. I told him to stop NOW, and he wasn't going to talk to her that way, and then it got into an ugly verbal battle. I do mean on and on, and he grabbed me. He had his hand around my neck and told me he was going to have his friends kill me. I don't know where I got the courage, but I looked him square in the eye and said, "QUIT SPITTING ON ME!"

He looked at me and stepped back. I guess he was shocked that I stood up to the lowlife. Joyce is sitting there numb! I think that was all she had. She did nothing to stop him or save me. For sure SHE HAD THE RIGHT TO BE TREATED BETTER, but I think that was her life. Thank God for the times in my life from birth to this moment he protected me from living in her hell. If she had kept me, my life would be a living hell.

So I called my sister from Chicago to come get me, and I spent the night with them. The next day I met George and Tom without Joyce. We had a great talk, and I told them what happened and how evil he is. They looked at each other, and I knew I was protected. They knew exactly what he was and his connections.

We continued to talk and learn about our lives. He told me about his family, and I told him about mine and mom and dad, Roger, the kids, the farm, and shared years and life. I was going home on the bus the next day. Tom wanted to take me home, and when we walked someplace, they were on each side of me. Protected. I told Tom I would be okay, but now I wish I would have. He could have seen our farm and met Roger and the kids.

They drove me to my sister's, and we said our goodbyes. I never saw Tom again. George came once to our farm, and of course, the kids were at camp for a week. But he saw our farm and met Roger, and we had a special time. He gave me a beautiful vase from Greece, and I treasure it. He called once in a while, and it was good. I knew what I was about and how I am, and the things I do that I didn't even know until I met him. It is so strange how we inherit ways and actions that we don't even know. It isn't all about who raised you, it's also about what came with you when you were born.

When I was 29 was an interesting year. We saw the King Tut exhibit in Chicago at the Field Museum. We drove to downtown Chicago and got our tickets. We were one of the last groups to go in. It was amazing. Roger and I were just in awe of the beautiful items and how they made such amazing things. The ancients were beyond craftsmen.

I also went to Norway that September with my mom and sister. We stayed with my aunt Dagne and Tone. I encourage her to go see her family. I told her SHE HAD A RIGHT to go and see her family. The last time mom saw her family was when she and Dad went there after they were married. And when her parents passed, she couldn't go because she had everyone to take care of. I remember how she cried and was alone in her grief. I tried to comfort her the best I could as a little girl. So she got our tickets, and we were going to Norway. That was in 1977. Jenny was two and a half. I got a girl who was family to come and stay to take care of the kids, and the farming went on.

So off to Norway we went, and I met family I had never known. I met other family, and it was a special time with all and a special time for mom to see her sister, brothers, and her parents' grave, shop in Norway, and be with her family. My other cousin, Wather, and his wife Marit had come and stayed with them, as well as Yngve and Gunn. What a great time. I had my 30th birthday in Norway. They bought me a Norwegian sweater. Marit came and picked me up, and I went to Oslo and stayed there for a while. We went to a fashion show and also went to my cousin's band, the Firebeats, and heard them play.

So that was a very interesting year, to say the least. I slid from 29 to 30 in a very interesting and special way.

He Is Gone

I hadn't heard from George for a few years now, and I knew something was wrong. I just had to find out what. I went to Chicago with my cousin (sister), Susan, and we went on the hunt. As we went by this certain cemetery, she said, "A lot of Greeks are buried there." I started to cry and said, "I hope he didn't die on my birthday." We went back to the cemetery. People are there during the day at the big cemeteries. We went into the office and I asked them if George was buried there. The head man asked me, "Who wants to know?" They knew him, and are very clannish of their people. I said, "His daughter, whether you like it or not." I was trying not to cry.

He gave us a map and told us where he was. Now I had my answer. The one I didn't want. We went to where he was and then I also went to his folks' (my grandparents) grave and I gave them my respects. We returned back to the building, and the head man asked me how long I was going to be in town. I said a couple of days. He said, "Come back tomorrow, I have someone I want you to meet."

It's the next day, and Susan and I are getting ready to go back to the cemetery, and I said, "We have to go and get a yellow rose." I have no idea why, but it just came to me. So we went to a florist on the way, and I got this most beautiful yellow rose. We got to the cemetery, and this wonderful lady came over and asked me if I was Charlene, and I said I was, and she had us come into her office.

It's amazing how God sends angels when you need them the most. We talked for about two hours, and she knew George. Her husband and George were friends. They played baseball when young, she told me many things, and I shared with her my family and my life, and it was good. I guess I HAD THE RIGHT to know, and I treasured our time together. I told her I had a yellow rose to put on his wall in the mausoleum. She said they don't usually want people to do that. Then she gave me the tape to put it on and said go. I taped it on, and it was beautiful.

When we took the tape back, we talked a little more and hugged each other, and I hold her in my heart and love her. She called a couple of times and we talked. Talk about a gift. She truly was one.

He died four days before my birthday.

The Medium and Me

After George's death, I felt like he was looking through my eyes when I was looking at something. Yes, I know, very strange. It would not be anything in particular, just a flower, grocery list, the yard, or whatever. There was something there, and I didn't know what or why. I talked to my daughter about it. She knew of this good medium. I had never done this before and wasn't sure I believed them, but I thought I would try once. So we made the appointment. I stayed the night with her in Madison, and in the morning, Jenny was sputtering about how she was mad at the way the Greek family was when I tried to get in touch with them, and I shouldn't be treated that way. I HAD THE RIGHT TO BE TREATED BETTER. I told her it didn't matter anymore.

We went to the medium, and she had us sit in the room. She told Jenny she had to sit and not say anything during this time. The medium asked why I was there. I gave her no hints. I said I just wanted to see what was out there, and I said no more. She was quiet for a few minutes and then said there was a man who wanted to come forward and wanted to know if it's okay. I said yes, it was.

She started telling me things that no one knew except for me. And the conversation went on to me as a little girl, and that George did see me before I was an adult. It was things that only I knew and things I didn't know before. She said George and I are very close and in tune with each other. She gave the example: if you took a rope and stretched it out straight, not a ripple or a bend, that is how in tune we are with each other. As we were doing this, she said, "There is another man who is older and wants to come forward." I said it was okay, and it was George's dad. Remember, I went to pay my respects at his and his wife's grave. She said he was looking at me, and then George and he said he always knew there was something, but didn't know what. Now he knows, and he was motioning his arms and welcoming me to the family. WOW. The other Wow was that George said thank you for the yellow rose. As we finished our session, the medium turned to Jennifer and said George wants you to know he liked your spunk this morning. Wow again.

I thanked her for this, and I never had the need to do this again. I had peace, and I sometimes think of him and mom and dad, Joyce, Helen, Dell, great grandpa, and great grandma, and all who have gone before and know that their love is with me yet. I come from Viking kings and queens and the ancients of Greece, where democracy started.

The combination is amazing. I love both cultures, what they have to offer, and the beauty of both countries.

PAIN AND PRIDE THEY BLEND SO WELL

Cancer

I am retired now and enjoying life with family and friends, doing some subbing at school and traveling. I had this cough and thought I had bronchitis. I went to the doctor, and he gave me an X-ray. Thank God for a good doctor. Yes, I had a spot on my lung. Years of smoking will do that. I had quit once and went to class to quit, and did well. But you always find an excuse to start again.

So now MY LIFE has changed drastically!

My doctor got me into an oncologist quickly, and she was wonderful. The test began right away. She was wonderful and an excellent doctor. When she told me I had cancer, I said giddy-up, let's get rid of it. So we did giddy up. Cancer changes your life and how you look at everything. And it affects the family and friends along with you. Everything seems to have a different look. A blade of grass, your home, friends, the farm, flowers, everything! I took a walk around our farm and into the woods, with a thankful feeling of what we had and what beauty was all around me that I never REALLY saw before.

Yes, believer, I quit smoking immediately with no problem. I have never desired it again. For all the people who started smoking when young because everyone did, it's not cool. It's SLAVERY and takes away everything you love.

Just remember YOU HAVE A RIGHT to have a good life and not slavery. Now I'm going for tests and going to fight this cancer with all I have. I also have friends with cancer, and one had lung cancer at the same time I did. We talked and shared our life with and about cancer.

I got so much support from friends and family. The cards came every day, and friends came over and brought food and gifts. Some people who I helped in their troubles in life did not even call. Amazing that they didn't care. Now true colors and empty people show.

The POWER of prayer is huge and beyond measure. Roger and the kids suffered along with me. It changes everyone's lives. The moments when you have cancer change your life with amazing things that you can't explain. I was going out from the grocery store in town when a lady said I THINK YOU NEED THIS, and she put an angel made from a bead on a string into my hand. As I turned around to thank her, she was GONE! Now for over a month, I was having tests and getting ready to get rid of the cancer. Another miracle moment was two days before I was to have surgery. I was out mowing the yard. I knew I wouldn't be doing it anymore that summer. I was in front of our old granary when all of a sudden, I felt the prayers circling me! I stopped the lawnmower and just embraced the powerful prayers. I raised my arms to God and asked him to hear them and let me be here for Roger and the kids and grandkids and to enjoy more life.

It was beyond beautiful, and I KNEW I was going to be okay, and God GAVE ME THAT

RIGHT to live. That was a moment I will never forget and can't even really explain! But you never forget those moments and are changed forever.

Rog was by the door one day with tears and said he couldn't live without me. I said, "I'll be here. I'm not done torturing you." I didn't want him to think I would let this cancer get us.

So the day has come, June 6, 2013. I had surgery. Before my surgery, the minister came in and prayed with us, and the doctors came in and asked me if I had any questions. I said, "No, I'm going to be okay." My surgeon was wonderful, and the care I had was excellent at Mercy Hospital in Oshkosh. This is a major surgery. They go from the back to front, and you're cut pretty well. Painful is an understatement.

I was in ICU for about four days and then moved to another room. The flowers and gifts from people coming to see me were more than wonderful. The nurses were so wonderful, and I will never forget them.

Now the day came I could come home! There is no place like home. And again, the food, cards, and people coming to see me. I have no words that can ever express my appreciation for friends and family. My one neighbor came once a week and cleaned. Just amazing. Roger cooked, cleaned, did laundry, and took care of me. I didn't lay in bed for over six weeks and had to sleep sitting up. My side was extremely sore. I couldn't lie down for over six weeks and had to sleep sitting up or in a recliner. Finally, I could sleep in a bed.

Roger had to make sure my medicines were taken at the right time and correctly.

A few weeks later, I had to go to have chemo. So every few weeks we went, and Jenny was there with us, and our daughter in law did so much for us too. Caretakers do not have it easy by any means, and they are often overlooked at the price of cancer. Again, life had changed for all of us. But we all learned a lot about so many things.

Now I'm healing and starting to wean myself off the drugs that can be so addictive. I knew what would happen if I didn't.

Lost Friends

The one friend who had cancer at the same time I did lost her battle with it. We talked about her journey, and I went to see her two days before she passed. I held her hand and talked to her about who she would see and what we had discussed. She smiled. I told her I loved her and I would see her again. Her daughter told me that was the last time she smiled. I went to another friend who had been fighting cancer for years and was in the nursing home. She was so happy for me, knowing she would not live much longer.

I have never forgotten what they gave me, and I had survivor's guilt for a long time.

I was asked to be the speaker at RELAY FOR LIFE the next summer. I had never done anything like that before, but I wanted to get my message out to people. It had rained, so we had to have it in the gym. The bleachers were full, and people's support was amazing.

I opened with: *Life isn't about waiting for the storm to pass, it's about learning to dance in the rain.* Instead of talking about me and my cancer, I told them what to do for people with cancer. To bring food, visit, send cards, clean, and pray. I talked about my experience with the lady and angel at the grocery store and about the lawn mower experience of the prayers. I talked about the ones who passed that year and what we shared. I wanted to give hope and knowledge of the power of prayers and what to do for people and families at that time and thanked everyone for the amazing support I had. I GOT A STANDING OVATION FROM THE CROWD!

When I was done, I had so many come up and thank me. One I will never forget is a young mom who had a daughter fight cancer, and she had the same angel given to her at the same store and was so glad I mentioned that. Her beautiful daughter was with her. How amazing! Oh yes, AMAZING GRACE.

Now when I know of someone with cancer, I do not take for granted or forget what people did for me. I have helped with benefits for cancer with friends and my daughter too. I find some of the people I gave to and helped forgot about me, and I find them to be empty people and have nothing to do with them. Because they have proven to me what they really are. Very sad they choose to go that way. But you go help whoever you can, and pray and support and LOVE.

Bucket List

You always hear about the bucket list and put it off. After my cancer, part of the change was this! You don't get another chance at life.

I always wanted to go to Athens, Greece, the other side of me. So we did. We went to Greece, and I went up to the Parthenon to see where I came from. George was Athenian

Greek. Not easy with COPD, but I did it. I made up my mind to, and I did just fine. The beauty of the ancients is beyond measure. I am always in awe of what the ancients have done and the beautiful buildings and things they have made. It makes you wonder HOW they did it. The talent and craftsmanship has stood the test of time.

We climbed on Mars rock, and I stood on the Acropolis looking over all of Athens and thinking about how far back all of this goes and the generations of Greece. I stood by the Parthenon and said George, I made it! We went to Corinth, Greece. The ruins were just beautiful. The museum had findings of things they dug up in Corinth! The robes draping off the statues looked like cloth, and the pillars were one big piece of stone to the sections like in Athens. How did they do it with no power tools and no big machinery to get the tons and tons of stone up? I have no words for the beauty that is still giving.

We went to Crete and Mykonos, saw more of beautiful Greece, shopped, and enjoyed the people. I was in one shop and talking with a young woman, and by the time we were done we hugged goodbye. I will never forget her.

We went to the Holy Land, Israel. That was another amazing experience. Again, the ancients and the Bible. Sailed on the sea of Galilee, went to the Garden of Gethsemane, the Church of the Holy Sepulchre, and the place of the crucifixion of Christ. The pillars inside are alabaster carved from the Crusades. We went to the River Jordan and also into Bethlehem. We were so lucky to go to Magdala, where in 2007, they were digging and found the synagogue Mary

Magdalene went to. A new find and beautiful first century Synagogue. A coin minted in 29 AD has the impression of Jesus teaching in the synagogue. Again walking with the ancients.

When you walk in the Via Della Rosa (the way of sorrow), the route Christ walked with the cross, you stop at the stations he had to stop at and try to wrap your head around what it really was like. But you can't. But now, when they talk about it, you know how it looks and have it with you.

We went to Rome, Italy, and again, we were just amazed at the beauty beyond description. Rome is just so beautiful, you can't put the ancient beauty into words. I'm always so thankful to the countries and how they respect and preserve their ancient history. We went to Naples, where pizza was first made. We were in a place from the 1700s that made this for Queen Margherita who came to Naples, and they made what is now known as pizza. She loved it, thus the name.

We went into a castle there, and again were amazed.

We went to Pompeii! Again the beauty has no words. The roads had ruts in them from the chariots, the color and murals on the walls were still there, the structures and the ancient beauty are now dug up and survived the ash from centuries of being buried. And they still are digging and finding things and more of Pompeii. The mosaics are still there and just stunning! What a treasured time.

We have traveled to beautiful places in the USA. Our country has beauty and is so great to see. Hilton head, Smoky Mountains, Oregon, North and South Carolinas, Virginia, New England, Tennessee, Missouri, Mississippi, Louisiana, Florida, Kentucky, Hawaii, South Dakota, and so much more

Last July, 2022, we went to Norway. I had been there but not for years. My cousin's daughter was an exchange student for a semester and spent Thanksgiving with us. So we had Thanksgiving and Christmas with her. What a special time for all of us.

A few years later, she was getting married in July and wanted us to come. We got our ticket and had plans to see family and Norway, the land of the Vikings and beauty beyond words. This was all new to Roger and some of it for me too. We went to Oslo and climbed on the roof of the opera house, saw the Munch art museum of work by the artist, Munch, the painter of "The Scream," and so much more of his beautiful work and other artists. We went to the Viking Museum by Oslo Fjord and saw the Viking burial mounds and ancient artifacts from the Vikings and the rune writings from the ancients. We saw Oslo and spent time with my cousin Yngve and his wife Gunn and got to see their son Espen, and Katja, and Christine and her family. Special memories.

We took a bus to Sogndal on Sognja Fjord and saw waterfalls, snow on the mountains, and reindeer crossing the road in front of us. Now the beauty was just again beyond words. We spent time with the family and saw beautiful Sogndal and the fjord. We went to the Selseng farm that has been in our family since the 1600s. They make this wonderful goat cheese, the brown Norwegian cheese. They were making it when we were there. So good. She was cooking it down with a wood fire and said it would take all day to make. It was beautiful with the mountains and waterfalls, the goats in the pasture, and the farm making hay.

We had a wonderful meal with Olav and Bjorg and met more family. We had a special treasured time that I know will never happen again. Not far from Selsegn farm is the Glacier museum, which was just beyond words. My cousin, Anna Mor, remembers in her lifetime when the Glacier was down to the lake. She and they know the world is changing.

We then went to Bergen, which is an ancient city with ancient buildings and just a beautiful old city. We climbed in a castle from the 1100s and went up the tram to the top of a mountain that overlooked Bergen. We went to the wedding in this old church that was so simply beautiful and spent the day with the whole family and met new people. We stayed with the bride's family and had the best time. The bucket list was filled with love from all of these people.

They all were so wonderful to us, and we all treasured our time together.

It was very hard to say goodbye because we all knew we wouldn't see each other again. That always makes my heart sad. They all were so wonderful to us, and Norway is in my heart and my family, who I love. But what a special last time to be together, and we hold it in our hearts that goes right to the soul. I have ancient Viking history that someone sent me, and we come from Viking kings and queens. The Viking ship in the museum is from our lineage. Wow.

I Love Miracles

have written about a few miracles in my life, and I realize that from my birth and on to this very day, I have had divine protection. There have been other miracles, and I will just mention a couple more. Remember Joyce trying to do the best she could do, My foster mother Helen, who was a blessing, my great grandfather, who was ahead of his time. He made crosses for churches, and they still are on the churches. He's still giving. He is the man who said SHE HAS A RIGHT to her family. I remember mom and dad, who all had strong faith. And I remember George, the other side of me. Sometimes strong faith is very judgemental, and I don't have the answer to any of it. I just know how it affected me in my life and the amazing journey I have had.

Another miracle in our family was when Roger was working on our car, a Lincoln that we bought used because it had good back seats to take mom and dad places as they needed. Roger was home alone, under the car, working on it. It fell on him, and he was pinned under it. He couldn't move and could feel himself dying. He prayed, and the car moved, and he got out from under it. He got to the house and called my friend Barb to come and take him to the doctor. There were no cell phones then. I had just come home when Barb was there, and they told me what happened. I took Rog to the doctor, and he was amazed.

Roger told me of his feeling of dying, and I will never forget what he told me: "Dying is easy, leaving my family is the hardest."

Farming is one of the most dangerous jobs there is, and again there had to be divine intervention. Our son Paul, who was about seven or eight at the time, was by the gate of the cow yard when all the cows got out and started to run and stampede out of the gate. Paul was there in the way. I couldn't get to him! I froze with fear. Now all 80 cows were out, and Paul was standing there scared but okay. All the cows went around him, and he was not hurt or dead.

Another time I was hauling the chopper box full of hay with a tractor up a hill, when the box started pulling the tractor backward down the hill with my son John on the tongue of the tractor. I couldn't stop it, and I was standing on the brake to try to stop it, and I couldn't stop it! I yelled, "Hang on, John! Just hang on no matter what." Then it jackknifed and stopped. My son was fine.

Our daughter was in a bad car accident. I got the call, and I didn't know if she was alive or not. Again the fear of what we may find. She and the other person were okay. Hurt but alive. Again when I saw it, I knew the kids were protected by angels. We were so thankful for both of them. She was in casts on her legs and in a wheelchair for a while.

She had so much support from friends, and her friends came out, and the house was full of love.

There was a dance at school, and she was in her wheelchair. Her friends came and got her to take her to the dance. While at the dance, a boy who she was always nice to but who had a rougher side of life and wasn't in high standards with others, came over and asked Jenny to dance, and of course, she couldn't. He got on his knees and danced with her. What a kind heart he had. He passed a few years later. It's amazing how someone who has lead a very wild life and is from the other side of the tracks had been so kind and left a mark on our lives.

We never know what is really inside of someone or the hurt they have. Terrible things happen, but with that, all lessons are learned, and love prevails. What we do and what we give is the key to it all. If your light is too bright for others, then it's they who are in the dark.

I saw this the other day, and it is the breath of life!

In Hebrew, YHWH represents breathing sounds. YH inhale WH exhale. So a baby's first cry calls his name. The breath of life. So even an atheist does it unaware.

Joyce, for all her trials, the angels were there in my birth and her passing. I have had an amazing life and have learned so much, and I hope to learn more, give more, share more, and love more.

But SHE HAD THE RIGHT was truly a gift from the start.

About the Author

CHARLENE STRATTON, author of *She Has A Right,* was born in a Salvation Army home in Chicago to an unwed woman. She was adopted by her grandparents and raised in a small town in Waushara county in the town of Wautoma, Wisconsin. Her journey is a story of coming from judgment to finally realizing that you have value; of learning through years of change and great experiences to become stronger and more determined not to give yourself away to negativity and to rise above jealousy. She is a cancer survivor, and the experience caused her to look at everything in her life differently, and to treasure family, friends, the miracles that life brings, and the time to never go back. Forgiveness heals and love endures. Now is the time for women to rise, value themselves, and support each other.

I want to support women in all their journeys.
Don't give yourself away, and don't let ANYONE
take your value away!

Made in the USA
Monee, IL
18 September 2023

42955637R10036